READING AND WRITING HANDBOOKS

PHONICS PATTERNS

EDWARD FRY, PH.D.

CB

CONTEMPORARY BOOKS

a division of NTC/CONTEMPORARY PUBLISHING GROUP
Lincolnwood, Illinois USA

ISBN: 0-8092-0879-2

Published by Contemporary Books,
a division of NTC/Contemporary Publishing Group, Inc.,
4255 West Touhy Avenue,
Lincolnwood (Chicago), Illinois 60712-1975 U.S.A.
0 1 2 3 4 5 6 7 8 9 VL 13 12 11 10 9 8 7 6 5

CONTENTS

Note: Rhymes (vowel sound plus consonant pattern) are alphabetical within the above vowel sound groups. For an alphabetical listing of rhymes, see page 63.

PREFACE

This is both a new and an old approach to teaching phonics for reading instruction.

It is old because *phonograms*, or *word families*, have been taught for decades through games and word wheels or, more formally, as word lists on chalkboards and charts. The basis of many work sheets, phonograms are also used as incidental instruction. For example, when a student has trouble sounding out an unknown word that contains a phonogram, the teacher not only points out the phonogram but also shows several other words that contain the same rhyme pattern.

Phonogram word lists are not a new idea, having been used in the *New England Primer* and *Webster's Blue Back Spelling Books* centuries ago. The lists presented here are refined, updated, expanded, and more accurate in vowel pronunciation. In fact, this is perhaps the largest, most complete listing of phonograms in existence.

The approach to teaching phonics is new in that the terminology is new. The terms *onset* and *rhyme* are used by today's linguists to illustrate something basic about a syllable. Although most of these lists look exactly like phonograms, let's explore them within the concept of onset and rhyme.

A *syllable* is defined as a vowel sound (vowel phoneme) with or without attached consonants. Most syllables have a consonant sound at the beginning and at the end, with a vowel in the middle. You can, however, omit one or both consonants. For example, *go* has no final consonant and is both a word and a syllable; the final syllable (*o*) in *po-li-o* has neither a beginning nor a final consonant sound.

In addition, the beginning consonant sound may actually be a blend of two or three consonant sounds, e.g., *stop*. Linguists call this beginning consonant sound the *onset* and the following vowel or vowel-plus-end consonant(s) the *rhyme*.

WORD		ONSET		RHYME
CAT	=	C	+	AT
BLACK	=	BL	+	ACK
GO	=	G	+	O

Furthermore, linguists determined that the break between the onset and the rhyme is a more natural one than the break between the vowel and the end consonant. There is, then, at least a theoretical justification for analyzing syllables using an onset and rhyme division rather than by breaking up each syllable into individual phonemes. Many classroom instructors agree with this practice, which probably accounts for decade after decade of teaching phonograms.

The word lists in this book contain only one-syllable words; there are, however, many polysyllabic words that contain the same onset and rhyme patterns. For example, note the *-ink* in *think* and *unthinkable* or the *-in* in *begin*.

Other new terminology might discuss rhymes as *spelling patterns*, a term that is also correct. Some people shun the idea of teaching single-phoneme phonics (*c* + *a* + *t*), instead preferring to talk about patterns like the *-at* found in *c* + *at* and *h* + *at* and the changing consonant as *consonant substitution*. A term related to *pattern* is *letter cluster*, although this term often refers to several sounds found together on many occasions. Examples include consonant blends, such as *bl* or *st*.

There are several ways, therefore, to analyze written language. Discussion of language theory and changes in terminology have limited practical application; there remains the business of teaching students to read and spell. These lists of word families were designed to help reach that goal in any way teachers and tutors may find useful.

PHONICS DISCUSSION

There are two main systems of writing. Most languages use an alphabet, a set of symbols that more or less represent the sounds of speech. English falls into this category.

A few languages use a system of ideographic symbols, in which a symbol stands for a concept. Chinese falls into this category. A person who lives in south China, therefore, cannot communicate by telephone with someone living in north China because the two speak different languages. They *can*, however, understand letters written to each other and are able to read the same newspaper. Another problem with the ideographic system of writing is that it is difficult to learn, and it takes a lot of instruction time. It is easier to learn to read and write an alphabetic language.

English uses an alphabet (set of symbols) originally designed for Latin. The match between the written letter and the spoken sound, therefore, is far from ideal because of changes in spoken English over the centuries. In addition, many words used in English come from other languages with variant spellings or use of symbols.

Yet, a good deal of correspondence still exists in English between the spoken sound and the written symbol. Various methods of trying to teach and understand this correspondence is what instructors call *phonics*. Linguists call it *phoneme-grapheme correspondence*. Phonics is taught as part of reading to help students "sound out" unfamiliar words; it is taught as part of spelling to help students correctly write the words they are learning.

Traditional phonics instruction tends to follow the method of individual sound connected to its spelling; each sound in a word is taught. For example, *cat* has three sounds, /k/, /ă/, and /t/; and *boy* has two sounds, /b/ and /oi/. This method has been highly effective in teaching beginning reading and writing. Phonics is not the only teaching method that can, or should, be used with beginning readers and writers, but it should be at least part of the method chosen.

This book presents one approach to phonics, not a complete knowledge of sound-spelling (phoneme-grapheme) correspondence. It contains phonics patterns, or particular combinations of letters that make certain sounds. More specifically, it contains onset and rhyme patterns. As discussed in the preface, an *onset* is the beginning consonant sound(s), and a *rhyme* is the following vowel-plus-consonant sound(s).

Although these patterns are not a complete course in phonics, they remain a highly effective way of teaching considerable phonics knowledge. They are also in harmony with virtually any single-sound phonics system, supplementing almost any method of phonics instruction. These patterns teach a lot about single consonant sounds and spellings of various vowel sounds.

PHONICS DISCUSSION

For those who may never have had reading instruction in English, working with these patterns also enhances something called *phoneme awareness*. *Phoneme awareness* is the internal realization that words are made up of discrete and interchangeable sounds. Phoneme awareness might also be regarded as readiness for learning how to read or for more formal phonics instruction.

At first, learning phonics might seem like quite a difficult job. In English there are somewhere between thirty-nine and forty-four different sounds (phonemes), depending on the linguist or dictionary consulted as an authority. All of these sounds are also spelled (written) using several hundred different letter combinations. For example, long /a/ is spelled *ai* in the word *aid*, *a-e* in the word *made*, or *ay* in the word *say*.

Yet, most people learn a great deal of phonics, whether or not it is taught formally, because phonics patterns are so prevalent in the English writing (spelling) system. Many teachers and educational researchers have found that phonics instruction, especially with beginning readers and writers, *does* facilitate learning how to read and how to spell.

In that spirit, I offer you more than 320 phonics patterns—the raw material for teaching phonics. For a more complete phonics system—a traditional phonics (or phoneme-grapheme) system of both common and uncommon correspondences—study the charts in Appendix 2. Most of these correspondences are illustrated with real words from the phonics patterns in this book.

—Edward Fry

TEACHING SUGGESTIONS _____

This book is a teaching tool—the raw material to be included as part of a reading or spelling lesson in adult literacy and ESL programs. Reading and spelling lessons are sometimes interchangeable—one helps the other. Use these phonics patterns in any way that works: as direct formal instruction, incidental learning, as a supplement to other phonics lessons, or even for speech correction. The Phonics Pattern Diagnostic Test (Appendix 1) on pages 55–56 can help you assess students' needs.

Here is a variety of lessons that incorporate the phonics patterns presented in this book.

Word Charts

-ab	-ag
cab	bag
dab	gag
gab	lag
jab	jag

Put a list or two on a chalkboard or chart. Have the student occasionally write the list or make the chart. Have the class, a small group of students, or individuals read the list. Discuss the words by using them in a sentence or saying something about their meaning. Feel free to omit obscure or unsuitable words; the purpose is to learn the pattern (rhyme) and to use various consonants (onsets) with it.

Select patterns for the lists that tie in with other spelling or reading lessons taught, taking care to introduce only one or two at a time to beginning students.

Select lists in any order, e.g., doing all of the short vowels first, then the long vowels. Or, do all of the short vowels first and select less common or more difficult groups later. These groups nicely illustrate the idea that the same sound can be spelled in different ways, if that is a teaching objective chosen.

Individual Lists

In a one-on-one situation or in a classroom setting, have the student write his or her own list for study. Letting one student teach another helps them both. You can duplicate a page of this book for individual study in class. Better yet, have students work selected exercises from *Phonics and Whole Words Activity Books 1* or *2*, the student skillbooks in the Reading and Writing Handbooks series designed to accompany this teacher text.

Spelling Lessons

The lists are also ideal for spelling lessons. A student who feels apprehensive on hearing that there will be twenty words on a spelling test may be relieved to learn that half of these words fall into an *-ack* pattern of such words as *back*, *hack*, and *Jack*, and that the other half follows a similar pattern.

Cards

An easy-to-make teaching aid is onset and rhyme activity cards. Put all of the onsets (beginning consonants) on small cards, and put a number of copies of the rhyme on other cards. The student tries to match cards to make real words. For an additional challenge, you can mix several groups together to make matching the cards more difficult, or add onsets that do not make real words. Another, fancier, way to make the cards is to use one card color or one color of ink marker for onsets and a different card color or ink for rhymes.

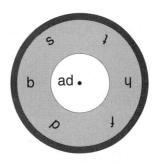

    The cards can also be used in a game. Students take turns drawing cards from a pile. When they have two cards that together make a real word, they score a point.

Word Wheels and Slip Charts

Word wheels show the rhyme printed on the smaller wheel on top and show onsets printed around the edge of the larger wheel behind it. New words are formed by turning the larger wheel. A student favorite because of its unique presentation, the word wheel provides the repetitive practice necessary for learning.

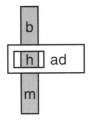

Slip charts are similar to word wheels in concept but are long and narrow. Show a rhyme on a card with a slot cut out on the left side. Put onsets on a strip narrower than the card slot and slide the strip through the opening of the rhyme card, as you would a buckle, to make a word.

Write a Poem

People enjoy poems that have end rhymes. Relevant examples of poetry can inspire students to have some fun writing rhymes of their own using a pattern like *-ay* and words like *May*, *jay*, *day*, and so on. If appropriate, you might even extend the concept of end rhymes by pointing out that *-ay* has the same sound as in *-ey*-pattern words, such as *hey* and *they*.

TEACHING SUGGESTIONS _____

Riddles

If you never have fun with words now and then during lessons, things can get pretty dull. Try getting students to develop some word riddles, using a rhyming pair of words in answer to a question. For example:

What is an overweight feline?	a fat cat
What is a strange rabbit?	a rare hare
What is an entrance to a shop?	a store door

As suggested for writing rhymes, you can mix pattern families to illustrate similar sounds:

What is the most important airplane?   the **ma**in **pl**ane

You get the idea—and you and your students can do even better!

Phoneme Awareness

An important goal of teaching phonics is for the student to realize that words are made up of specific sounds (phonemes), that these same few sounds come up in many different words, and, finally, that these sounds are spelled either in only one way or in more than one way—which is the essence of phonics.

Learning onset and rhyme patterns helps develop phoneme awareness by showing students that just changing the beginning consonant sound can form new words. Such instruction can be given orally as an introduction to a reading or spelling lesson.

Speech Correction

Students who do not speak English as their first language often have trouble pronouncing all of its phonemes because some of these languages do not contain all of the phonemes used in English. Spanish, for example, has no /j/ sound; the Spanish word *general* sounds like *heneral* to speakers of English. Certain Asian languages, such as Japanese, have no /l/ sound; native speakers of that language usually pronounce the word *luck* as *ruck*.

Non-native English speakers can improve their English pronunciation by practicing selected phonics patterns. When working with such students, it is important to remove any emotional pressure by not placing them in an embarrassing position and to remember that speech sound production is purely mechanical, learned through repetition. Students can often observe such mechanical problems as incorrect tongue placement for a certain sound in English simply by watching themselves make the sound in front of a mirror, then watching the teacher or tutor make the same sound. Once students observe the correct placement of the tongue to form a certain sound, they can gradually substitute the new speech pattern for the old one through practice speaking words with the troublesome sound.

Incidental Instruction

Some instructors do not like formal or scheduled phonics lessons, preferring instead to teach phonics as the need occurs. The phonics patterns in this book can greatly enhance this incidental way of teaching phonics. For example, tell the student how to spell a word when she asks, but also point out the word's phonics pattern and that it is spelled the same as the pattern in five other words, one or two of which she may already know. This approach is also a good way to extend a student's word and spelling knowledge.

SHORT a SOUND

Dictionary Phonetic Symbol: Thorndike /a/, Webster /a/

-ab

cab
dab
gab
jab
lab
nab
tab
blab
crab
drab
flab
grab
scab
slab
stab

-ack

back
hack
Jack
lack
Mack
pack
sack
tack
black
clack
crack
knack

shack
slack
smack
snack
stack
track
whack

-act

fact
pact
tact
tract

-ad

bad
cad
dad
fad
had
lad
mad
pad
sad
tad
Brad
Chad
clad
glad

-aff

chaff
staff

-aft

daft
raft
waft
craft
draft
graft
shaft

-ag

bag
gag
hag
lag
nag
rag
sag
tag
wag
brag
crag
drag
flag
shag
snag
stag
swag

SHORT a SOUND

-am
cam
dam
ham
jam
Pam
ram
Sam
tam
yam
clam
cram
dram
gram
scam
scram
sham
slam
swam
tram

-amp
camp
damp
lamp
ramp
vamp
champ
clamp

cramp
scamp
stamp
tramp

-an
ban
can
Dan
fan
man
pan
ran
tan
van
bran
clan
flan
plan
scan
span
than

-ance
dance
lance
chance
France
glance
prance

stance
trance

-anch
ranch
blanch
branch

-and
band
hand
land
sand
bland
brand
gland
stand

-ang
bang
fang
gang
hang
pang
rang
sang
clang
slang
sprang

-ank

bank
dank
hank
lank
rank
sank
tank
yank
blank
clank
crank
drank
flank
Frank
plank
prank
shank
spank
thank

-ant

pant
rant
chant
grant
plant
scant
slant

-ap

cap
gap
lap
map
nap
pap
rap
sap
tap
yap
chap
clap
flap
scrap
slap
snap
strap
trap
wrap

-ash

bash
cash
dash
gash
hash
lash
mash
rash
sash
brash
clash
flash
slash
smash
stash
thrash
trash

-ask

ask
cask
mask
task
flask

-asm

chasm
plasm
spasm

-asp

gasp
hasp
rasp
clasp
grasp

Short a Sound

-ass
bass
lass
mass
pass
brass
class
glass

-ast
cast
fast
last
mast
past
vast
blast

-at
bat
cat
fat
gnat
hat
mat
pat
rat
sat
tat
vat
brat
chat
flat
scat
slat
spat
that

-atch
batch
catch
hatch
latch
match
patch

-ath
bath
math
path
wrath

-ax
lax
Max
tax
wax
flax

Hat

Long a Sound

Dictionary Phonetic Symbol: Thorndike /ā/, Webster /ā/

-ace
face
lace
mace
pace
race
brace
grace
place
space
trace

-ade
bade
fade
jade
made
wade
blade
glade
grade
shade
spade
trade

-age
cage
gage
page
rage
sage

wage
stage

-aid
laid
maid
paid
raid
braid
staid

-ail
bail
fail
Gail
hail
jail
mail
nail
pail
rail
sail
tail
wail
flail
frail
quail
snail
trail

-ain
lain
main
pain
rain
vain
brain
chain
drain
grain
plain
slain
Spain
sprain
stain
strain
train

-aint
faint
paint
saint
taint
quaint

-aise
raise
braise
chaise
praise

-ait
bait
gait
wait
strait
trait

-ake
bake
cake
fake
Jake
lake
make
rake
take
wake
brake
drake
flake
quake
shake
snake

-ale
bale
dale
gale
hale
male
pale

sale
tale
scale
shale

-ame
came
dame
fame
game
lame
name
same
tame
blame
flame
frame
shame

-ane
bane
cane
Jane
lane
mane
pane
sane
vane
wane
crane
plane

-ange
mange
range
change
strange

-ape
cape
gape
nape
rape
tape
drape
grape
scrape
shape

-ase
base
case
vase
chase

-aste
baste
haste
paste
taste
waste
chaste

-ate
date
fate
gate
hate
Kate
late
mate
rate
crate
grate
plate
skate
slate
state

-ave
cave
Dave
gave
pave
rave
save
wave
brave
crave
grave
shave
slave
stave

-ay
bay
day
gay
hay
jay
lay
may
nay
pay
ray
say
way
bray
clay
cray
fray
gray
play
pray
quay
slay
spray
stay
stray
sway
tray

-aze
daze
faze
gaze
haze
maze
raze
blaze
craze
glaze
graze

-eak
break
steak

-eigh
neigh
weigh
sleigh

-ey
hey
prey
they
whey

Sleigh

Broad a Sound

Dictionary Phonetic Symbol: Thorndike /ä/, Webster /ä/

-ar
bar
car
far
jar
mar
par
tar
char
scar
spar
star

-ard
card
guard
hard
lard
yard
shard

-arge
barge
large
charge

-ark
bark
dark
hark
lark
mark
park
Clark
shark
spark
stark

-arm
farm
harm
charm

-arn
barn
darn
yarn

-arp
carp
harp
tarp
sharp

-art
cart
dart
mart
part
tart
chart
smart
start

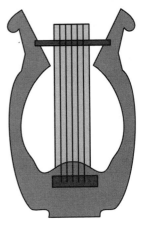

Harp

SHORT e SOUND

Dictionary Phonetic Symbol: Thorndike /e/, Webster /e/

-air

air
fair
hair
lair
pair
chair
flair
stair

-are

bare
care
dare
fare
hare
mare
pare
rare
ware
blare
flare
glare
scare
share
snare
spare
square
stare

-ead

dead
head
lead
read
bread
dread
spread
thread
tread

-ealth

health
wealth
stealth

-ear

bear
pear
wear
swear

-eck

deck
heck
neck
peck
check
fleck
speck
wreck

-ed

bed
fed
led
Ned
red
Ted
wed
bled
bred
fled
Fred
shed
shred
sled
sped

-edge

hedge
ledge
wedge
dredge
pledge
sledge

SHORT e SOUND

-eft
deft
heft
left
cleft
theft

-eg
beg
keg
leg
Meg
peg

-eld
held
meld
weld

-ell
bell
cell
dell
fell
hell
jell
knell
Nell
sell
tell
well
yell
dwell
quell
shell
smell
spell
swell

-elp
help
kelp
yelp

-elt
belt
felt
knelt
melt
pelt
welt
dwelt
smelt

-em
gem
hem
stem
them

-en
Ben
den
hen
Ken
men
pen
ten
yen
glen
then
when
wren

-ence
fence
hence
pence
whence

-ench
bench
wench
clench
drench
French
quench
stench
trench
wrench

-end

bend
end
fend
lend
mend
rend
send
tend
vend
wend
blend
spend
trend

-ense

dense
sense
tense

-ent

bent
cent
dent

gent
Kent
lent
rent
sent
tent
vent
went
scent
spent

-ep

pep
rep
prep
step

-ept

kept
wept
crept
slept
swept

-esh

mesh
flesh
fresh

-ess

Bess
guess
less
mess
bless
chess
dress
press
stress
tress

-est

best
guest
jest
lest
nest
pest
rest
test
vest
west
zest
blest
chest
crest
quest
wrest

SHORT e SOUND

-et
bet
get
jet
let
met
net
pet

set
wet
yet
Chet
fret
whet

-etch
fetch
retch
sketch
wretch

-ex
hex
sex
vex
flex

-ext
next
text

Jet

LONG e SOUND

Dictionary Phonetic Symbol: Thorndike /ē/, Webster /ē/

-e

be
he
me
we
she

-ea

pea
sea
tea
flea
plea

-each

beach
leach
peach
reach
teach
bleach
breach
preach

-ead

bead
lead
read
knead
plead

-eak

beak
leak
peak
teak
weak
bleak
creak
freak
sneak
speak
squeak
streak
tweak

-eal

deal
heal
meal
peal
real
seal
teal
veal
zeal
squeal
steal

-eam

beam
ream

seam
cream
dream
gleam
scream
steam
stream
team

-ean

bean
dean
Jean
lean
mean
wean
clean
glean

-eap

heap
leap
reap
cheap

-ear

dear
fear
gear
hear
near
rear

Long e Sound

-ear (cont.)

sear
tear
year
clear
shear
smear
spear

-east

beast
feast
least
yeast

-eat

beat
feat
heat
meat
neat
peat
seat
bleat
cheat
cleat
pleat

-eath

heath
sheath
wreath

-eave

heave
leave
weave
cleave
sheave

-ee

bee
fee
knee
lee
see
tee
wee
flee
free
glee
tree

-eech

beech
leech
breech
screech
speech

-eed

deed
feed
heed
need

reed
seed
weed
bleed
breed
creed
freed
greed
speed
steed
tweed

-eek

leek
meek
peek
reek
seek
week
cheek
creek
Greek
sleek

-eel

feel
heel
keel
kneel
peel
reel

-eel (cont.)
creel
steel
wheel

-eem
deem
seem
teem

-een
keen
seen
teen
green
preen
queen
screen
sheen

-eep
beep
deep
jeep
keep
peep
seep
weep
cheep
creep

sheep
sleep
steep
sweep

-eer
beer
deer
jeer
leer
peer
seer
queer
sneer
steer

-eet
beet
feet
meet
fleet
greet
sheet
skeet
sleet
street
sweet
tweet

-eeze
breeze
freeze
sneeze
squeeze
tweeze
wheeze

-ief
brief
chief
grief
thief

-ield
field
yield
shield

Deer

Short i Sound

Dictionary Phonetic Symbol: Thorndike /i/ Webster /i/

-ib
bib
fib
jib
rib
crib
glib

-ick
Dick
hick
kick
lick
Nick
pick
Rick
sick
tick
wick
brick
chick
click
flick
quick
slick
stick
thick
trick

-id
bid
did
hid
kid
lid
rid
grid
skid
slid

-iff
miff
tiff
cliff
skiff
sniff
whiff

-ift
gift
lift
rift
sift
drift
shift
swift
thrift

-ig
big
dig
fig
gig
jig
pig
rig
wig
brig
sprig
swig
twig

-ilk
bilk
milk
silk

-ill
bill
dill
fill
gill
hill
ill
Jill
kill
mill
pill

-ill (cont.)

sill
till
will
chill
drill
frill
grill
quill
skill
spill
still
swill
thrill
trill
twill

-ilt

gilt
jilt
hilt
kilt
tilt
wilt
quilt
stilt

-im

dim
him
Jim
Kim
rim
Tim
vim
brim
grim
prim
slim
swim
trim
whim

-imp

limp
chimp
crimp
primp
skimp
blimp

-in

bin
din
fin

gin
kin
pin
sin
tin
win
chin
grin
shin
skin
spin
thin
twin

-ince

mince
since
wince
prince

-inch

inch
cinch
finch
pinch
winch
clinch
flinch
Grinch

SHORT i SOUND

-ing
bing
ding
king
ping
ring
sing
wing
zing
bring
cling
fling
sling
spring
sting
string
swing
thing
wring

-inge
binge
hinge
singe
tinge
cringe
fringe
twinge

-ink
kink
link
mink
pink
rink
sink
wink
blink
brink
clink
drink
shrink
slink
stink
think

-int
hint
lint
mint
tint
glint
print
splint
sprint
squint

-ip
dip
hip
lip
nip
rip
sip
tip
zip
blip
chip
clip
drip
flip
grip
quip
ship
skip
slip
snip
strip
trip
whip

-ish
dish
fish
wish
swish

Short i Sound

-isk

disk
risk
brisk
frisk
whisk

-isp

lisp
wisp
crisp

-iss

hiss
kiss
miss
bliss
Swiss

-ist

fist
list
mist
wrist
grist
twist

-it

bit
fit
hit
kit
knit
lit
pit
sit
wit
flit
grit
quit
skit
slit
spit
split
twit

-itch

ditch
hitch
pitch
witch
switch

-ive

give
live

-ix

fix
mix
six

Switch

Dictionary Phonetic Symbol: Thorndike /ī/, Webster /ī/

-ibe
jibe
bribe
scribe
tribe

-ice

bride
chide

glide
pride
slide
snide
stride

-ie
.e
e
.e
e
e

-ed
.ed
ed
ied
ried
ied
ied
ied

-er
ier
ier
ier

-ies
dies
lies
pies
ties
cries
dries
flies
spies

-ife
fife
knife
life
rife
wife
strife

-igh
high
sigh
nigh
thigh

-ight
fight
knight
light

LONG i SOUND

-ight (cont.)

might
night
right
sight
tight
blight
bright
flight
fright
plight
slight

-ike

bike
dike
hike
like
Mike
pike
spike
strike

-ild

mild
wild
child

-ile

bile
file
mile
Nile
pile
tile
vile
smile
while

-ime

dime
lime
mime
time
chime
clime
crime
grime
prime
slime

-ind

bind
find
hind
kind
mind
rind
wind
blind
grind

-ine

dine
fine
line
mine
nine
pine
tine
vine
wine
brine
shine
shrine
spine
swine
twine
whine

Long i Sound

-ipe
pipe
ripe
wipe
gripe
snipe
stripe
swipe

-ire
fire
hire
tire
wire
spire

-ise
rise
wise

-ite
bite
kite
mite
rite
site
quite
white

-ive
dive
five
hive
jive
live
chive
drive

-uy
buy
guy

-y
by
my
cry
dry
fly
fry

ply
pry
shy
sky
sly
spy
spry
sty
why

-ye
bye
dye
eye
lye
rye

Fire

Short o Sound

Dictionary Phonetic Symbol: Thorndike /o/, Webster /ä/

-ob

Bob
cob
gob
job
knob
lob
mob
rob
sob
blob
glob
slob
snob

-ock

dock
hock
knock
lock
mock
rock
sock
tock
block

clock
crock
flock
frock
shock
smock

-od

cod
God
mod
nod
pod
rod
sod
clod
plod
prod
shod
trod

-og

bog
cog
dog

fog
hog
jog
log
tog
clog
flog
frog
grog

-oll

doll
loll
moll

-omp

pomp
romp
chomp
stomp

-ond

bond
fond
pond
blond

SHORT O SOUND

-op	-ot	-otch
bop	cot	botch
cop	dot	notch
hop	got	blotch
mop	hot	crotch
pop	jot	Scotch
sop	knot	**-ox**
top	lot	ox
chop	not	fox
crop	pot	lox
drop	rot	pox
flop	tot	
plop	blot	
prop	clot	
shop	plot	
slop	shot	
stop	slot	
	spot	
	trot	

Stop

LONG O SOUND

Dictionary Phonetic Symbol: Thorndike /ō/, Webster /ō/

-o

go
no
so
pro

-oach

coach
poach
roach
broach

-oad

goad
load
road
toad

-oak

soak
cloak
croak

-oal

coal
foal
goal

-oam

foam
loam
roam

-oan

Joan
loan
moan
groan

-oast

boast
coast
roast
toast

-oat

boat
coat
goat
moat
bloat
float
gloat

-obe

lobe
robe

globe
probe
strobe

-ode

code
lode
mode
node
rode
strode

-oe

doe
foe
hoe
Joe
toe
woe

-ogue

rogue
vogue
brogue

-oke

coke
joke
poke
woke

LONG O SOUND

-oke (cont.)

yoke
broke
choke
smoke
spoke
stoke
stroke

-old

bold
cold
fold
gold
hold
mold
old
sold
told
scold

-ole

dole
hole
mole
pole
role
stole
whole

-oll

poll
roll
toll
droll
knoll
scroll
stroll

-olt

bolt
colt
jolt
molt
volt

-ome

dome
home
Nome
Rome
tome
chrome
gnome

-one

bone
cone
hone

lone
tone
zone
clone
crone
drone
phone
prone
shone
stone

-ope

cope
dope
hope
mope
pope

-ose

hose
nose
pose
rose
chose
close
prose
those

Long o Sound

-ost
host
most
post
ghost

-ote
note
quote
rote
vote
wrote

-ove
cove
wove

clove
drove
grove
stove
trove

-ow
bow
know
low
mow
row
sow
tow
blow
crow
flow
glow

grow
show
slow
snow
stow

-own
known
mown
sown
blown
flown
grown
shown

Rose

Short oo Sound

Dictionary Phonetic Symbol: Thorndike /ů/, Webster /ů/

-ood

good
hood
wood
stood

-ook

book
cook
hook
look
nook
took
brook
crook
shook

-oor

boor
poor
moor
spoor

-oot

foot
soot

-ould

could
would
should

-ull

bull
full
pull

Book

Long oo Sound

Dictionary Phonetic Symbol: Thorndike /ü/, Webster /ü/

-ew
dew
few
hew
Jew
knew
new
pew
blew
brew
chew
crew
drew
flew
grew
slew
stew
threw

-o
do
to
who

-oo
boo
coo
goo

moo
too
woo
zoo
shoo

-ood
food
mood
brood

-oof
goof
roof
proof
spoof

-ool
cool
fool
pool
tool
drool
school
spool
stool

-oom
boom
doom
loom
room
zoom
bloom
broom
gloom
groom

-oon
boon
coon
goon
loon
moon
noon
soon
croon
spoon
swoon

Long oo Sound

-oop

coop
hoop
loop
droop
scoop
sloop
snoop
stoop
swoop
troop

-oose

goose
loose
moose
noose

-oot

boot
hoot
loot

moot
root
toot
scoot
shoot

-ooth

booth
tooth

-ooze

booze
ooze
snooze

-oup

soup
croup
group

-ube

cube
lube
tube

-ude

dude
nude
rude
crude
prude

-ue

cue
due
hue
Sue
blue
clue
flue
glue
true

-uke

duke
nuke
puke
fluke

Long oo Sound

-ume	**-use**	brute
fume	fuse	chute
flume	muse	flute
plume	ruse	**-uth**
-une	**-ute**	Ruth
June	cute	truth
tune	lute	
prune	mute	

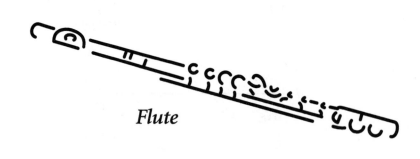

Flute

BROAD O SOUND

Dictionary Phonetic Symbol: Thorndike /ô/, Webster /ȯ/

-alk
balk
talk
walk
chalk
stalk

-all
ball
call
fall
gall
hall
mall
pall
tall
wall
small
squall
stall

-alt
halt
malt
salt

-aught
caught
naught
taught
fraught

-aunch
haunch
launch
paunch
staunch

-aunt
daunt
gaunt
haunt
jaunt
taunt
flaunt

-aw
caw
gnaw
jaw
law
paw
raw

saw
claw
draw
flaw
slaw
squaw
straw

-awl
bawl
brawl
crawl
drawl
shawl
scrawl
trawl

-awn
dawn
fawn
lawn
pawn
yawn
brawn
drawn
prawn

BROAD O SOUND

-oar

boar
roar
soar

-ong

bong
dong
gong
long
song
tong
prong
strong
thong
wrong

-oor

door
floor

-orch

porch
torch
scorch

-ord

cord
ford
lord
chord
sword

-ore

bore
core
fore
gore
more
pore
sore
tore
wore
chore
score
shore
snore
spore
store
swore

-ork

cork
fork
pork
York
stork

-orm

dorm
form
norm
storm

-orn

born
corn
horn
morn
torn
worn
scorn
shorn
sworn
thorn

BROAD O SOUND

-ort
fort
Mort
port
sort
short
snort
sport

-oss
boss
loss
moss
toss
cross
floss
gloss

-ost
cost
lost
frost

-oth
moth
broth
cloth
froth
sloth

-ought
bought
fought
ought
sought
brought

-our
four
pour

Sport

oi SOUND

Dictionary Phonetic Symbol: Thorndike /oi/, Webster /ȯi/

-oil	**-oint**	**-oy**
boil	joint	boy
coil	point	coy
foil	**-oist**	joy
soil	foist	Roy
toil	hoist	soy
broil	moist	toy
spoil		ploy

-oin

coin
join
loin
groin

Coin

Dictionary Phonetic Symbol: Thorndike /ù/, Webster /aù/

-ouch
couch
pouch
vouch
crouch
grouch
slouch

-oud
loud
cloud
proud

-ounce
bounce
pounce
flounce
trounce

-ound
bound
found
hound
mound
pound
round

sound
wound
ground

-our
hour
sour
flour
scour

-ouse
douse
house
louse
mouse
rouse
souse
blouse
grouse
spouse

-out
bout
gout
lout
pout

rout
tout
clout
grout
scout
shout
snout
spout
sprout
stout
trout

-outh
mouth
south

-ow
bow
cow
how
now
row
sow
vow

-ow   (cont.)

brow
chow
plow
prow

-owl

fowl
howl
jowl

growl
prowl
scowl

-own

down
gown
town
brown
clown

crown
drown
frown

-owse

dowse
browse
drowse

Crown

SHORT u SOUND

Dictionary Phonetic Symbol: Thorndike /u/, Webster /ə/

-ome

come
some

-on

son
ton
won

-ough

rough
tough
slough

-ove

dove
love
glove
shove

-ub

cub
dub
hub
nub
pub
rub
sub

tub
club
flub
grub
scrub
shrub
snub
stub

-uch

much
such

-uck

buck
duck
luck
muck
puck
suck
tuck
Chuck
cluck
pluck
shuck

stuck
struck
truck

-ud

bud
cud
dud
mud
crud
spud
stud
thud

-udge

budge
fudge
judge
nudge
drudge
grudge
sludge
smudge
trudge

-uff
buff
cuff
huff
muff
puff
bluff
fluff
gruff
scuff
sluff
snuff
stuff

-ug
bug
dug
hug
jug
lug
mug
pug
rug
tug
chug

drug
plug
shrug
slug
smug
snug
thug

-ulk
bulk
hulk
sulk

-ull
cull
dull
gull
hull
lull
mull
skull

-um
bum
gum
hum
mum

rum
sum
chum
drum
glum
plum
scum
slum
strum
swum

-umb
dumb
numb
crumb
plumb
thumb

-ump
bump
dump
hump
jump
lump
pump
rump

Short u Sound

-ump (cont.)
chump
clump
frump
grump
plump
slump
stump
thump
trump

-un
bun
fun
gun
nun
pun
run
sun
shun
spun

-unch
hunch
lunch
munch
punch
brunch
crunch

-ung
dung
hung
lung
rung
sung
clung
flung
slung
sprung
stung
strung
swung
wrung

-unk
bunk
dunk
funk
hunk
junk
punk
sunk
chunk
drunk
flunk
plunk

shrunk
skunk
slunk
spunk
stunk
trunk

-unt
bunt
hunt
punt
runt
blunt
grunt
shunt
stunt

-up
cup
pup
sup

-us
bus
pus
plus
thus

-ush

gush
hush
lush
mush
rush
blush
brush
crush
flush
plush
slush
thrush

-uss

buss
fuss
muss
truss

-ust

bust
dust
gust
just
lust
must
rust
crust
thrust
trust

-ut

but
cut
gut
hut
jut

nut
rut
Tut
glut
shut
smut
strut

-utch

Dutch
hutch
clutch
crutch

-utt

butt
mutt
putt

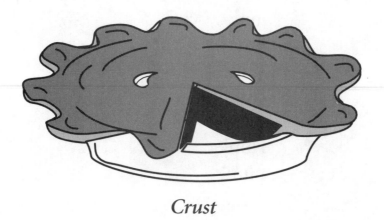

Crust

ur SOUND

Dictionary Phonetic Symbol: Thorndike /ėr/, Webster /ər/

-earn
learn
yearn

-erb
Herb
Serb
verb

-erge
merge
serge
verge

-erk
jerk
perk
clerk

-erm
germ
term
sperm

-ern
fern
tern
stern

-erse
terse
verse

-erve
nerve
serve
verve
swerve

-ir
fir
sir
stir
whir

-ird
bird
gird
third

-irk
quirk
shirk
smirk

-irl
girl
swirl
twirl
whirl

-irt
dirt
flirt
shirt
skirt

-irth
birth
girth

-ur	**-url**	**-urse**
cur	burl	curse
fur	curl	nurse
blur	furl	purse
slur	hurl	**-urt**
-urk	**-urn**	curt
lurk	burn	hurt
murk	turn	blurt
Turk	churn	spurt
	spurn	

Phonics Patterns
Diagnostic Test

This test will help you quickly find the phonics development level of any student. Simply ask the student to read the nonsense word in each category below. Note on a separate sheet of paper or a copy of this test where errors are made and then teach the patterns in those categories. The categories (vowel sounds) below match the categories on pages 12–54 of this book. Nonsense words in each vowel category have either an easy (or common) rhyme pattern or a harder (less common) rhyme pattern. If the student recognizes or knows the rhyme (vowel plus final consonant), he or she should be able to sound out each nonsense word.

Sound	Easy Patterns	Harder Patterns
Short /a/	mab fam	thasp sance
Long /a/	jace baint	shaze crange
Broad /a/	dar mard	tharge narp
Short /e/	jed ket	threlp betch
Long /e/	ree geat	smief scheave
Short /i/	pib gligh	stisp trinch
Long /i/	pice kile	drize phie
Short /o/	pob bot	swomp trox
Long /o/	moe goke	skown flost
Short /oo/	dook nood	brould froor
Long /oo/	poot mue	thew floup

Sound	Easy Patterns	Harder Patterns
Broad /o/	nall lork	chought quawl
/oi/	noil croy	wroist foin
/ou/	jour fout	shouse kounce
Short /u/	pum grunk	lough sudge
/ur/	hern surn	zirl slurse

Notes

It is not necessary to do the whole test in one sitting. Test a few categories, take a break, teach to discover students' needs, then test additional categories later.

Certain vowel spellings can have more than one sound. For example, *ea* is a short /e/ in *bread* but a long /e/ in *seat*. Just explain that the same sound can be spelled in different ways. Encourage the student to use the sound you are testing. As you teach these word (phonogram) families, the various spellings (letters) for the same vowel sound will become readily apparent.

PHONICS CHARTS ──────────────── APPENDIX 2

VOWEL SOUNDS
(alphabetical order)

Phoneme		Common Spelling	Less Common Spelling
short /a/	/ă/	**a** hat	
long /a/	/ā/	**a–e** age, **ai** aid	**eigh** eight, **ay** say, **ey** prey
broad /a/	/ä/	**a** (**r**) far	**a** father
short /e/	/ĕ/	**e** red	**ea** head
long /e/	/ē/	**e** repay, **ee** see	**ea** seat, **y** lazy
short /i/	/ĭ/	**i** bit	**y** gym
long /i/	/ī/	**i–e** ice, **y** try, **i** child	**ie** pie
short /o/	/ŏ/	**o** hot	**a** watch
long /o/	/ō/	**o** so, **o–e** nose	**oa** boat, **ow** know
broad /o/	/ô/	**o** (**r**) for, **o** loss	**a** (**l**) all, **a** (**u**) auto, **a** (**w**) awful
/oi/, /oy/	/oi/	**oi** boil, **oy** boy	
/ou/, /ow/	/ou/	**ou** out, **ow** owl	
long /oo/	/o͞o/	**oo** moon	**u** ruby, **ew** chew, **o** do, **ou** soup, **u–e** duke
short /oo/	/o͝o/	**oo** good	**u** (**l**) pull, **ou** could
short /u/	/ŭ/	**u** nut	**o** son
long /u/	/ū/	**u–e** use, **u** music	
ə Schwa	/ə/	**a** alone, **e** taken, **i** direct, **il** pencil, **ou** generous, **o** riot, **u** campus	
		(Some dictionaries say that the schwa phoneme is the unaccented vowel sound, so it must appear in a polysyllable word. Others say that schwa and short /u/ are the same.)	
Schwa + *r*	/ər/	**er** her, **ir** sir, **ur** fur	

VOWEL SOUNDS
(clustered)

Short Vowels

a-at /ă/
e-end /ĕ/
i-is /ĭ/
o-hot /ŏ/
u-up /ŭ/

Long Vowels Open Syllable Rule

a-baby /ā/
e-we /ē/
i-idea /ī/
o-so /ō/

Long Vowels Final *e* Rule

a-make /ā/
e-eve /ē/
i-five /ī/
o-home /ō/
u-use /ū/

Long Vowel Digraphs

ai-aid /ā/
ay-say /ā/
ea-eat /ē/
ee-see /ē/
oa-oat /ō/
ow-own /ō/

Schwa

u-hurt /ə/
e-happen /ə/
o-atom /ə/

Vowel *y*

y-try /ī/
y-funny /ē/

Vowel plus *r*

er-her /ʉr/
ir-sir /ʉ/
ur-fur /ʉ/
ar-far /är/
or-for /ôr/

Diphthongs

oi-oil /oi/
oy-boy /oi/
ou-out /ou/
ow-how /ou/

Double /o/

oo-soon /o͞o/
oo-good /o͝o/
u-truth /o͞o/
u-put /o͝o/

Broad /o/

o-long /ô/
a (l)-also /ô/
a (w)-saw /ô/
a (u)-auto /ô/

Vowel Exceptions

ea-bread	/e/	In a few words, *ea* stands for the short /e/ sound.
e (silent)-come		In a few words, final *e* does **not** make the preceding vowel long.
y-yes	/y/	*y* is a consonant at the beginning of a word.
le-candle	/əl/	final *le* represents the sound of schwa plus /l/.
al-pedal	/əl/	final *al* represents the sound of schwa plus /l/.
il-pencil	/əl/	final *il* represents the sound of schwa plus /l/.
ul-awful	/əl/	final *ul* represents the sound of schwa plus /l/.

CONSONANT SOUNDS
(alphabetical order)

Phoneme	Common Spelling	Less Common Spelling
/b/	**b** boy	
[c]	(no *c* phoneme; see /k/ and /s/)	
/ch/	**ch** cheese	**t** nature
/d/	**d** dog	
/f/	**f** fat	**ph** phone
/g/	**g** girl	
/gz/	**x** exert	
/h/	**h** hot	
/j/	**j** just, **g** giant	
/k/	**c** cat, **k** king	**ck** sick, **ch** chrome
/ks/	**x** fox (no *x* phoneme)	
/kw/	**qu** quick (no *q* phoneme)	
/l/	**l** look	
/m/	**m** me	
/n/	**n** no	**kn** knife
/ng/	**ng** sing	
/p/	**p** put	
[q]	(no *q* phoneme; see /kw/)	
/r/	**r** run	**wr** write
/s/	**s** sit, **c** city	
/sh/	**sh** shut, **ti** action	**s** sugar, **ch** chute
/t/	**t** toy	
/th/ (voiced)	**th** this	
/th/ (voiceless)	**th** thing	
/v/	**v** voice	
/w/	**w** will	
/wh/	**wh** white	
[x]	(no *x* phoneme; see /ks/ and /gz/)	
/y/ (consonant)	**y** yes	**i** onion
/z/	**s** his, **z** zero	
/zh/	**si** vision	**su** pleasure, **ge** beige

CONSONANT SOUNDS
(clustered)

Single Consonants That Usually Stand for Specific Single Sounds

b	j	p	w
d	k	r	y
f	l	s	z
g	m	t	
h	n	v	

Consonant Digraphs That Usually Stand for Specific Single Sounds

ch as in *church*
sh as in *shoe*
th (voiced) as in *thin*
th (voiceless) as in *this*
wh (*hw* blend) as in *which*

Other Important Spelling-Sound Connections

c = /k/ before *a, o,* or *u* as in *car*
c = /s/ before *i, e,* or *y,* as in *city*
ch =/k/ as in *character*
ch = /sh/ as in *chef*
g = /j/ before *i, e,* or *y,* as in *gem*
ge = /zh/ as in *massage*
gh = /f/ as in *laugh*
i = /y/ as in *million*
ng = /ng/ unique phoneme, as in *sing*
ph = /f/ sound as in *phone*

qu = /kw/ blend as in *quick*
    (the letter *q* is never used
    without *u*)
s = /z/ as in *has*
s = /sh/ as in *sure*
si = /zh/as in *vision*
su = /zh/ as in *measure*
t = /ch/ as in *capture*
ti = /sh/ as in *attention*
x = /ks/ blend, as in *fox*
x = /gz/ blend, as in *exact*

Common Beginning Consonant Blends

br	bl	sc	scr	dw
cr	cl	sk	squ	tw
dr	fl	sm	str	
fr	gl	sn	spr	
gr	pl	sp	spl	
pr	sl	st	shr	
tr		sw	sch	
wr			thr	

Silent Consonants

gn = /n/ as in *gnat*
kn = /n/ as in *knife*
wr = /r/ as in *write*
igh = /i/ as in *right*
ck = /k/ as in *back*
mb = /m/ as in *lamb*
lf = /f/ as in *calf*
lk = /k/ as in *walk*
tle = /əl/ as in *castle*

Common Final Consonant Blends

ct-*act*	**lt**-*salt*	**nk**-*ink*	**rd**-*hard*	**sk**-*risk*
ft-*lift*	**mp**-*jump*	**nt**-*ant*	**rk**-*dark*	**sp**-*lisp*
ld-*old*	**nd**-*and*	**pt**-*kept*	**rt**-*art*	**st**-*least*

Although phonics instruction helps beginning readers and writers improve their skills, there is more to good reading and spelling than phonics. Here is a list of the 100 most common words used in English. It is nearly impossible to write a paragraph without using some of them. Because these 100 words make up half of all the words used in written English, students must be able to recognize (read) and write them (spell correctly) with little effort or hesitation. Note that many of the words are not phonetically regular. Teach them as whole words, using flash cards, spelling lessons, or bingo games. The complete list of high-frequency words appears in *1000 Instant Words*, the other teacher reference book in the Reading and Writing Handbooks series.

1–5	16–20	31–35
the	as	but
of	with	not
and	his	what
a	they	all
to	I	were

6–10	21–25	36–40
in	at	we
is	be	when
you	this	your
that	have	can
it	from	said

11–15	26–30	41–45
he	or	there
was	one	use
for	had	an
on	by	each
are	word	which

46–50
she
do
how
their
if

66–70
him
into
time
has
look

86–90
call
who
oil
now
find

51–55
will
up
other
about
out

71–75
two
more
write
go
see

91–95
long
down
day
did
get

56–60
many
then
them
these
so

76–80
number
no
way
could
people

96–100
come
made
may
part
over

61–65
some
her
would
make
like

81–85
my
than
first
water
been